WHY I AM A JEW

BY

EDMOND FLEG

TRANSLATED FROM THE FRENCH
BY
LOUISE WATERMAN WISE

WITH A FOREWORD BY
STEPHEN S. WISE

NEW YORK
BLOCH PUBLISHING COMPANY
"The Jewish Book Concern"
1933

DEDICATED

TO MY GRANDSON
who is not yet born

FOREWORD

From time to time Jewish books come out of France which arrest the attention of the Jewish world. Such a book was Darmesteter's *Hebrew Prophets,* the richness of the content equalled by the beauty of the style. Palliere's *Unknown Sanctuary,* not written by a Jew, came not very long ago as a revelation to those who had not heard of the thrilling quest of a sanctuary by one preparing, as he imagined, for the Catholic priesthood. Each of these a document of the first importance! The one an involuntary tribute by one Jewishly self-exiled, the other the passionately eager song of a soul finding home at the altar of Judea.

And recently another of the sons of French Jewry, Edmond Fleg, has renewed the unfading glory of the Franco-Judean literary tradition, which includes the immortal name of Rashi of Troyes. This glory seems to shine most brightly when Jewish life is at its darkest, for literature meaningful and rich is not so much the utterance of fullness of life, as the prophecy of a happier by a poorer age.

Why I am a Jew, by Edmond Fleg, belongs to

a series of little books published under the general
title, "Leurs Raisons." It is a chapter in an auto-
biography which includes "The Child Prophet" and,
strange though this may sound, "The Life of Moses."
For Edmond Fleg is another of the "Shomerim,"
watchmen upon the tower, prophets of an unex-
pected renaissance in one of the oldest and, as it
seemed, least vital of world Jewries, France.

Why I am a Jew is an atypical narrative of a
Jewish experience. The tale, written with Gallic
charm and Hebraic warmth for an unborn grand-
child, is of the life of a Jewish child reared in the
alienative atmosphere of an outwardly Orthodox
but basically unobservant Jewish home.

Comes the environment of secularism in school
and college, which in a dominantly Christian world
is deeply and pervasively Christian, and then
L'Affaire, the testing of France, though France knew
it not, by the Dreyfus trial; to France a test and for
some great Jews, such as Herzl, Nordau and Fleg,
revealing and cleansing. And yet for Fleg this was
not enough, and in the arena of his innermost life
battles remained to be fought, battles of the intellectual life, wars of the spirit with the tempting hosts
of doubt and cynicism. It was not easy to make his
way back to that which in essence lay behind him.
Escape tempted. Freedom beckoned. But the call of

truth was most imperious to his soul. And in the end he suffered no lesser considerations than those of truth to govern his decision to take his place once again with his people. Since his return, he has given much to his people's cause in a series of books, which are as vital as his re-born faith and his re-won loyalty.

While yet a very young man, Fleg became eye-witness in one of its earlier Congresses of the Zion-ist,—what shall we call it—movement or cataclysm. And Fleg, prepared by much that had gone before, found therein not so much reason as justification, not so much proof as prophecy of the ultimate faith that became his own. There are books which are called epochal because they give rise to epochs. *Why I am a Jew* is epochal in another sense, in sum-ming up an epoch in the life of Westernized, de-ghettoized Jews who think as humans, philosophize as Westerners, feel as Jews. Over and beyond the closely knit reasoning for the faith that is in Fleg, his is a lyrical exultation over the faith that, finding good, he longs to hand on to children's children. Mystic is his exaltation of a faith, which, because most simple and free from complexities and subtle-ties, allows fullest play for that direct, immediate, unimpeded access to the Truth of Truths, which is the religion of his people.

Aiming to be *apologia pro fide sua*, Fleg's book is an exultant witness to the undimmed radiance of Israel's faith and the unlessened persuasiveness of Israel's life. It is of the essence of romance, for it is a tale of nobleness and spiritual suffering, of chivalry and triumph. And while not untouched by the inherent pathos of his people's life, the Judenschmerz is subordinated to the Hallelujah of a joyously self-affirmant and self-liberated Jew.

STEPHEN S. WISE

New York, June 1929.

CONTENTS

INTRODUCTION

I am asked why I am a Jew. It is to you, my grandson who are not yet born, that I would make my reply.

When will you be old enough to understand me? My eldest son is nineteen years old My younger son is fourteen years old. When will you be born? In ten years, perhaps fifteen. . . . When will you read what I here set down? About 1950, 1960? Will people still read in 1960? What form will the world then take? Will the mechanical have suppressed the spiritual? Will the mind have created a new universe for itself? Will the problems that trouble me to-day exist for you? Will there be any Jews left?

I believe there will. They have survived the Pharaohs, Nebuchadnezzar, Constantine, Mohammed; they have survived the inquisition and assimilation; they will survive the automobile.

But you, my child, will you be a Jew? People say to me: You are a Jew because you were born a Jew. You did not will to be one; you cannot change that. Will this explanation suffice for you, if, born a Jew, you no longer feel that you are a Jew?

I myself, at the age of twenty, thought I had no further interest in Israel. I was convinced that Israel would disappear, that in twenty years people would no longer speak of it. Twenty years have passed, and twelve more, and I am again become a Jew—so obviously that I am asked why I am a Jew.

That which happened to me may happen to you also my child. If you believe that the flame of Israel is extinguished within you, pay heed and wait; some day it will be rekindled. It is a very old story, which begins anew each century. Israel has had a thousand opportunities to die; a thousand times it has been reborn. I want to tell to you how it died and was reborn in me, so that, if it die in you, you in turn may experience its rebirth.

Thus I will have brought Israel to you, and you will bring it to others if you will, if you can. And we two in our way will have treasured and transmitted the divine behest:—"These words which I command thee shall be upon thy heart and upon thy soul; bind them as a sign upon thy hand and let them be as frontlets between thine eyes. Thou shalt teach them to thy children. . . ."

"We are the heartbeat of a world that wills
To find its noblest self and to fulfill
The law of Justice which it seeks to know;
We are God's people, for we will it so,
The stars our quest and truth our watchword still!"

WHY I AM A JEW

CHAPTER I

ISRAEL LOST

I

In my childhood I saw things that no doubt you will never see My father was a Zaddik[1] following the Scriptures, and my mother the joyous priestess of her home. At that time religion was mingled with every act of life, but in so simple a way that I saw no religion in it.

I found it quite natural that in the morning my father enveloped himself in a white shawl with black stripes, and wound bands of leather about his forehead and his left arm, while murmuring words which were not mere words. The blessing after meals seemed as much of a necessity to me as the meal itself, and on Friday night there seemed nothing unusual in seeing my mother extend her hands, which had become transparent, over the wicks flickering in the oil.

All that governed the kitchen was hierarchically

[1] Hebrew word, meaning an utterly righteous person

1

regulated. One must not eat butter after meat, nor use a knife to cut the chicken which was to be used for cheese; two vessels were used, one for meat and the other for milk-foods, and to confuse them were a sin.

When a goose arrived from Strassburg it bore around its neck, upon a red seal, signs which fomented archaeological controversies around the kitchen sink, because it was important to my mother and to Lisette the cook, to establish by careful scrutiny at what hour of which day the animal had been bled, and if it were lawful to metamorphose it into delicious food.

Ham, oysters, crabs, game, had but a nominal existence; their taste was unknown to me, as were the color and form of these forbidden foods.

To have entered a tram-car on a Saturday would have seemed as venturesome as to ascend to the moon, and to blow out a candle on that day as unthinkable as to blow out the sun.

Certain rites—but what a ceremonious word for these familiar acts—returned each year as normally as did the seasons which they accompanied; there was the waving of the palm with a perfumed citron, or a row of lights on a board, arranged in decreasing sizes, which were lighted from the smallest to the tallest.

Once every year I ate alone at noon, and my brothers, who were old enough to fast, returned from the Synagogue with wan faces whose pride I admired.

At other times my mother and old Lisette went on a hunt into all the corners of our home, and into all the pockets of our clothes searching for crumbs. The round loaf on the table ceded its place to thin cakes without leaven. At dinner my father, his hat upon his head, chanted Hebrew melodies Bitter herbs and mortar were passed from hand to hand, four cups of wine were drunk, and the door was left open for someone who did not enter.

I did not understand what all this meant nor did I ask about it of others or of myself. I only felt one thing—that the faces of my parents had at these times a radiant joy and serenity that I have not seen since, except in the pictures of the greatest of the saints.

It was not only impure foods that were forbidden; other inhibitions forbade lying, laziness, gluttony, coarseness, spitefulness, every manner of evil; and the spirit of unity, of kindness and of love as obviously held sway as did the customary domestic acts. Morals were not discussed, rarely mentioned. They were practised. They were as much a part of life as were our daily habits. I never heard a word that was not tender and gentle between my parents.

To lie before them, to use an ill-sounding or querulous expression, would have been unthinkable. A gentle but firm justice punished our faults and rewarded our will to do well. The example of toil and of thrift taught us every hour of the day. Pleasure had its place but was not an end in itself. Charity was practised as a natural function. My father was frequently consulted, disputes were submitted to him, and so much of peace emanated from him that adversaries who came to consult him left our home reconciled. Perfect manners, goodness of heart and highmindedness illumined our very humble home to which one climbed by ascending a somber staircase.

Then there was God; we lived with God, but His presence was subconscious, never spoken of. I did not hear the mention of His name; I only uttered it during the evening prayer which my mother, or even Lisette, bade me repeat before tucking me into bed. It was a very brief prayer; a few words in Hebrew which I repeated without understanding their meaning, and then a single sentence: "God protect Father, Mother, and all those I love." Yes, it was a short prayer, and yet this it was which caused the undoing of my respect for the family-worship.

The light having been put out, I remained alone with the God to whom I had just recited a lesson. Then I spoke to Him. In what terms? In what language? How can I repeat it to you, my unborn grandson? If you in turn know these impulses toward the invisible, if you feel as I felt, this thrill from beyond, if you silently respond to this call from within, you too will find the words which came to me.

I knew God was present, very far away and yet quite close, all around me and in my heart. I told Him all my faults and I besought His forgiveness. I wanted to be better; I could not be without Him. I promised Him to do better, I implored Him to help me And He did help me, I am sure of it I rose to Him. He enveloped me. He held me. I fell asleep in His arms.

Who taught me to pray in this way? No one. But what were all the incomprehensible litanies and inexplicable gestures worth compared with this voiceless and formless prayer? I will try to write words which will lend my stammering thought the clarity it needs I began to feel a contrast between my prayer when alone, which was close to me, and the prayer of my father which I did not comprehend Or rather, mine only seemed to me to be a prayer, the other a habit that God did not notice.

My critical sense too began to grow. I did not write on Saturday at school. That was forbidden But at college my elder brothers wrote on that day just as on other days; their studies made it necessary.

My father went to his office on Saturday after synagogue services. He also wrote, his business made it
necessary. Was therefore the rest on the Sabbath-day
only important for very little boys?

Once I was taken on a journey, and at the hotel
where we dined the fat and the lean were mixed, and
cheese was served after meat, and even ham appeared
on the table. My parents ate and permitted me to
eat of this forbidden dish. Then the food forbidden
at home was no longer forbidden when one was away
from home? The law was law no longer?

Thus like all children of all time, I began despite
myself to scrutinize my parents, and drawing conclusions from their inconsistencies I very slowly began to break their idols.

Others unconsciously became my accomplices. The
first of these was my teacher of religion, the cantor
of the synagogue. He had a beautiful voice, a beautiful beard, a beautiful soul. But as a teacher he puz-
zled me. I was at this time attending college, and
was proud of my Latin. Now this man taught that
the Hebrew had *no grammar*, which caused me to
feel dubious about that language and what it inculcated Then too, his method alone would have dis-
couraged the most inquisitive of minds. I mumbled
prayers which he declared *untranslatable*. The cate-
chism began with a sentence which amused me:

"Who are you, my child? I am a young Jew or Jewess." As for the sacred history and the Psalter chanted by my illiterate cantor, how badly it sounded after my Greek or Roman history.

My father, who read Hebrew in the evenings, would say to me occasionally: "It is a very beautiful language." I did not think it was. How could I? Jewish values were poorly presented to me—knowledge gained at college alone counted.

And that which was begun by the ignorance of the cantor was continued by the cynicism of the Rabbi. Occasionally he came to visit us in the evening after dinner, and we took our seats again around the table, a glass of claret was poured for him, and we listened as he talked.

He had a shaven lip between his magisterial whiskers, and he was an enchanting conversationalist. The whole town doted upon his wit. Could I divine that his scepticism concealed his faith, and that he truly found joy in proclaiming the divine unity. To judge by the God who spoke to me at night, the caustic humor of his earthly representative seemed altogether too human.

Professor of Comparative Philology at the university, he scoffed disdainfully at the small traders of his community, whom however, upon every possible occasion he heartily served. If one were to believe him, the Jewish tailor, when he passed by his shop, felt of the cloth at the back of his rabbinic coat because he had bought it of the Christian tailor, and the cattle dealer, who sought a good match for his daughter, declared: "I am not a cattle dealer; I am a manufacturer of meat." There were some Jewish tales—amusing Jewish tales, over which I laughed but also blushed a little: the story of the two Jews who had dined at a restaurant and left the door open as they went out on a stormy night, and who muttered on hearing themselves abused from within: "Listen to the anti-semites," or of Moses, playing *écarté* with God in Paradise, saying: "Above all, God, no miracles."

This gallery of portraits and this collection of stories, pleasant as they were, marred Israel to my too sensitive soul. And I could not forget these grotesque pictures when I betook myself against my will to the Synagogue.

I was taken to the Synagogue for the first time according to custom when I was a very small boy, to roll up one of the sacred scrolls with a long linen band covered with colored letters. I wore my velvet suit with pearl buttons, and was in a state of elation, for from the height of the gallery my mother was watching me, and the gold stars painted in the blue ceiling seemed to me real stars in a real heaven.

But I had come to know the cantor and the Rabbi too well. They robbed the place of its illusions. And excepting for the rare moments which the music transformed, or when the hidden splendor of the ceremony suddenly burst forth in its manifest beauty, what boredom I felt in those dull hours, weighed down the more by the meticulous phrases of an unknown tongue!

What physical irritation I felt against those persons without breeding who read their newspapers or conversed aloud; what disgust when I heard the only words spoken in French, and these, in order to stimulate generosity, announcing under the eye of the Holy Law the amount given for charity by each donor.

At the age of thirteen years, when I "made my first Jewish communion," I could chant very well before the ark, without sounding a false note in the Biblical text of which I understood not one word, and in the evening after the festival I could recite in one breath the benediction which had remained Hebrew to me. But when I was alone at night in my bed, face to face with the God who came to me, I asked myself quite mystified if indeed He was the God of Israel.

He was, my child. All those prayers the meaning of which escaped me, magnificently revealed Him, all those ceremonies the emptiness of which gave me a sense of loneliness, emanated from His presence. But I knew it not—it was badly explained to me, and I was to wander a long time among men and thoughts before arriving at the truth.

Ah, you will say, this is a strange way of explaining to you why I am a Jew. But you will not understand why I am a Jew unless you first understand why I ceased to be a Jew.

In those early years of my adolescence the break was not yet conscious. But my spirit unconsciously turned away from the spirit of my people. And I was soon to discover another world.

II

In my fourteenth year I had overtaxed my strength. My best friend and classmate at that time, now a pastor and professor of theology, lived in the country. I was in need of fresh air; his mother desired to have me visit him. I played the piano and because of my love of music I was invited to a neighboring home, where I became a daily guest.

An old lady lived there with her daughter and three sons, two of whom were already grown men. Widow of a famous writer, she had known "Monsieur Taine," "Monsieur Renan," "Monsieur Got," and had traveled much in Italy. Her conversation was replete with memories. In my home there was great respect for intellectual culture; here one enjoyed familiarity with it.

The quite rustic dwelling faced a large meadow, which commanded a cliff where the Rhône turns in a rocky circle My elderly friend helped me to see in nature that which had never been pointed out to me. The play of clouds and the drama of light were events for her; they became events for me.

I did not quite understand just what seemed new to me in this home, but harmony reigned therein in a very different way from that I had known. Strange and tiresome though the religious customs (which chimed with the days, months, and years for us) had seemed to me, I never conceived of existence without them. But here were no dietary laws, no imperious rites, no oppressive prohibitions. One went to services on Sunday; that was all. And yet not quite all. Work, charity, the kindness which were merely practised in our home, were here consciously lived and helped one to achieve a clear conscience. The moral instinct was enriched and clarified by all the light that the living word could bring to it.

Then the mother, the brothers, the sister, were so detached from one another in their own definite interests! If there were a question concerning a walk, or blame or praise of any act, of a decision to be taken, however important, each one of them expressed his ideas as though it were permissible to have individual ideas. The ancestral community spirit which in our home imposed itself upon us would have hindered such divergencies. And dimly I felt myself rebelling against it.

I have since understood what was happening to me then. In Geneva, where I was born, the sects were strictly separated. I had no life other than the Jewish life. Our Ghetto was not shut in by chains, but none the less it was a Ghetto. I had come out of it for the first time I looked upon free air and a free sky, and my spirit liberated itself not only from the rites of the Jewish family but from the family itself.

The following winter a book took me still further away from Israel—the Gospel. It was not my friends who placed this formidable discovery before my eyes. Their sense of delicacy would not have permitted them to do this. But I, whom no one had known how to interest in the Old Testament, I wanted to know this Jesus who was preached to them on Sundays. I still see beneath the trees of the old square, the stand of the secondhand bookshop, where for a few centimes I bought all this revelation of suffering I still hear my heart cry out at the furtive reading of those eternal pages. I was the shepherd close to the cradle;

I was the fisherman of Tiberias; I walked with the paralytic; I again saw the light with the blind; I again came to life with Lazarus; "Our Father" was my prayer, the Sermon on the Mount was my sermon; the agony on the cross my agony. But at the end of my Passion, I did not murmur as did the Christ: "Forgive them, they know not what they do." No, I remember that crucified by horror and shame for my race, quite small and alone in my room I cried out "Dirty Jews, dirty Jews!"

I have told of my anguish at that time in *"L'Enfant Prophète."* [1] I do not wish to go over it again. But to show you that that story was not merely a ,romance and to make clear to you what I dared to call in those far off days "my religious thought," I will copy here, without any changes in its poor style, that which I then wrote in my diary and found last night among some old papers:

"I am not a believer; it is my old religion that is at fault, my poor religion, the ruin of an unfinished building. What care for forms; those absurd customs! Alas, laws against eating ham, against tearing paper on Saturday, the custom of eating bread without leaven for seven days, have long since caused my soul to

[1] A recent book by Edmond Fleg

rebel though I dared not confess it. The reading of the New Testament has finally detached me from all this. I have wept real tears while reading about the tortures of Jesus, and I have felt ashamed of my fathers who sullied themselves with the blood of this just man whom they so treacherously crucified. Yes, I am ashamed of my people. I have heard it said that a Jew and a Christian can never live in peace together. I am not a Jew, oh no!

It may be a despicable thing thus to put the faith of one's ancestors out of one's heart, but I do not feel that I must imitate their errors. My opinions are my own, no one has inculcated them within me I have read no books concerning them. I have heard it said that Christians alone can understand their religion, because their religion is the life of Jesus. It is also my religion because this life so radiant is the life that shall be my example; his charity, his mercy, are the objects of my admiration; these are what my soul loves and what it finds truly great.

I understand Jesus, but do not look upon him as a supernatural being; that is beyond my comprehension, and I cannot think him divine by closing my eyes; that were unworthy of my in-

telligence. But I can better understand Jesus
than I can understand a God, absolute master
and judge of all things. It is not that I am an
atheist, oh no! I say my prayers every night,
but I pray to a God within me who is not a ruler.
I have been told that God is a spirit. Why should
he not be the thought that makes its voice heard
in the conscience of each one of us? Perfect
faith, I admire it, I envy its possession but,
alas, I have it not. I cannot be a Jew. I can be
a Christian. And if I can follow him I have
chosen as my model, if I look upon the good
as God, and if I think he may be the revelation of
an omnipotent God, am I so very blameworthy?
May I be pardoned if I err, may I find mercy
above if I have doubted. God, let thy light enter
within me, reveal thyself to me if thou art."

Since that time I have reviewed the process of the
trial of Jesus and I hope that you my child, more
correctly informed, will never know the sorrow of
accusing your whole race—which was my first sorrow.

Yet this God of my prayers, the one gift and the
most precious which was left to me of Israel, this
God whom I already so coldly called the Good but
who so vitally dwelt within me that I still addressed

myself to him as to a living person, even this God was to forsake me.

It happened a year later and in the most trivial way. I was eager to become a philosopher, and there being no class in philosophy at Geneva I trusted myself without a guide to the thousand pages of a popular history of philosophy. At last I was to know. In haste I opened the big volume—first of all Religion— How was it that there were such varying ideas about God, and so many that were contradictory?

Of the God of Israel not one word; is He then unimportant? But I learn that a certain Protagoras wills to ignore whether there are Gods or not, and that a certain Critias maintains they were invented by a legislator as cautious as he was crafty. Socrates, I am told, revealed the moral God, the God of "civilized nations." Plato placed him in the "realm of ideas." Aristotle identified him as "the pure act," the Stoics confounded his unity with that of the universe, and Plotinus made of him a trinity. What was I to believe? Whom was I to follow? I was perplexed.

In the middle ages, the same disputations were translated into scholastic jargon. St. Augustine does not agree with St. Thomas, Averroes is not in accord with Scotus. In modern times the warfare continues;

Malebranche against Descartes, Leibnitz against Spinoza!

Of course, there were many evidences offered, the familiar evidences of the existence of God. But I had read too much; the evidences proved nothing to me. And how triumphant I felt when Kant arrived with his heavy club and pulverized all these affirmations. Oh, how well he spoke! How right he was! Yes, we impose upon things the laws of our own being, we cannot conceive of them in and of themselves; we know not the Being nor the Substance nor the Absolute, nor God.

Then Herbert Spencer came forward like a prestidigitator holding the doctrine of evolution in his hands. Three turns of his cuffs and I saw the One producing the Many, and the Simple producing the Complex, from the humblest atom of matter to the loftiest creation of the spirit. Twice presto chango, and by enchantment the vegetable emerged from the mineral and man from the animal! A little shove, and from Heredity and the Association of Ideas, suddenly these ancient illusions escape, Good, Evil, Freedom, God!

Finally Auguste Comte and his Positivism brought certitude to me. Humanity had evidently passed through three successive stages: in the theological period it explained natural phenomena by supernatural causes; wonders, miracles, were the acts of God. In the metaphysical period mankind had recourse to abstractions converted into realities, faculties, essence and accident; in the third period, the period that still obtains, we happily limit ourselves to knowledge thru observation and experimentation in the relationship of phenomena. This last method, the only one that is of value, has created modern science and has forever supplanted metaphysics and theology; there is no other religion than the Religion of Humanity; the problem is settled.

Upon this discovery of the great void an entire wall of my inner life collapsed. I should have perished but nothing happened. I was too proud of being a philosopher to complain of the errors that encompassed me. My nightly conversations with God changed in tone. The words, *Reveal thyself if thou art,* which I formerly repeated in my agony, were no longer a prayer; they were a summons. I defied this God, I blasphemed against Him. Then giving up the effort to obtain speech from the non-existent, I abandoned him and his silence.

Far distant as I was at this time from Israel, I was to take myself still further away. I went to Paris and entered the higher class of rhetoric, attended the Sorbonne and was admitted to the Normal School.

Here was material to help me to come to my senses, but the contrary happened. I wanted to combine for myself some austerity with much self-indulgence, but I must confess to you that toward my twentieth year I was soaring to a height of pretentiousness from which in the face of certain facts I was compelled to descend later on Seeming to be under the spell of what I chose to call my charm, some of my comrades amused themselves by forming a small circle about me, whose loyalty was tempered by raillery. We were called the *Aesthetes*, and I have a notion that this was not a misnomer. I leaned upon Anatole France and Renan, and had drawn from the pure springs of these two masters the sophisticated waters of my dilettantism, for we were dilettantes.

One must not take the world too seriously; one did not even know if it existed, for one left crass certitudes to the common people. Society was not worth the trouble of mingling with it. Of what importance to subtle spirits were eternal principles, the Rights of the Man and the Citizen, the battle of parties or the form of the state? Ethics also seemed very dull; Good and Evil were dumbells that one need not trouble to handle. Art alone counted, not only the art of words, sounds, forms and colors, accessible after all to inferior bipeds who could read a book, listen to a concert or walk thru a museum, but the art of creating from moments taken from one's own life an opus worthy of contemplation.

My chief function then was to admire myself, and as in the fluid mobility of my self-scrutiny it would have seemed a poor thing to admire but one person within myself, I distinguished at least five, each of which corresponded to one of my friends; there was Des Grieux who was bored by Tiberge, the Pylades of an ever bitter Orestes, the Agathon of a modern Socrates, the satirist who juggled with the shadow of things, and the romanticist whose piano endured in turn frenzies and ecstasies.

Could so complex a being inhabit this lowly earth without peril? Would not life in simplifying him cause him to perish? It was decided that such a misfortune must be prevented My Socrates was not terrified by one more hemlock story. He brought me a vial of seeming poison which however he had filled with pure water; otherwise you would never have had a grandfather.

Do not think, my child, that I illuminate the past for the unique satisfaction of evoking glittering memories If there be one quality—or one defect—commonly attributed to Israel, it is too great concern for this earthly existence. Idealist or materialist he clings to life, be it to exploit or to ennoble it. To turn away from it, to abdicate before his time, either in contemplation, in inaction or in death, is not the habit of the Jew. I had forsaken the rites and the laws of my people I had rejected their God; and the inmost voice of my people had grown silent within me.

CHAPTER II

ISRAEL REGAINED

I

I was in this state of mind when the tidings came that Captain Dreyfus, banished to Devil's Island as a traitor in 1894, had been unjustly condemned for the one and only reason that he was a Jew. At first the whole matter did not interest me. It was a news-item which could not disturb my contemplative life, and with the little thought that I consented to give it, I believed it unlikely that seven army-officers, because of mere *prejudice* could have sent an inno-cent man to hopeless imprisonment. It was incredible to me.

However, the agitation increased thruout the country in favor of the condemned man. Several of our teachers interested themselves in his case; soon he had defenders among my comrades in the school, even among the Aesthetes, and detached as I might be from worldly affairs, I in my turn was obliged to descend from my empyrean for him.

I had one close friend who was not a student of the
Normal Institute. We had come to know one another
in the last year of college, and were soon bound together by an affection that still endures. The deep
tenderness which united us was the attraction of an
altogether intellectual sympathy. Our greatest joy
was our mutual understanding, and the formulating
of our ideas in unison. I felt a certain pride in main-
taining this aspect of our friendship I did not want
it to consist of mutual acts of service which seemed
to me the current money of sentiment, nor of that
cheap confidence which expresses itself in the ex-
change of secrets. In fact, a sort of shyness separated our souls that were really so close to one another. The Dreyfus affair was to reveal the cause to
me.

He was brought up in an environment foreign to
every reactionary or even conservative tendency;
very sensitive, but of a sensitiveness without any
romanticism, and saturated with the destructive in-
difference which was that of Maurice Barrès in his
early years. He was highly intelligent and much more
endowed than was I with the force of logic; (we will
call him the *Logician*) and had accepted all the conclusions of our common nihilism.

If ever there was a loyal and a free spirit, it was
his; he had liberated himself from all philosophical

illusions; he had broken all social idols; even the love of fatherland had given way under his analytical keenness.

His overwhelming scepticism, contrary to mine, admitted from the beginning that the innocence of Dreyfus was eminently possible, but in the measure that the successive disclosures drew me closer to this hypothesis, to my great astonishment I saw his opinion develop in the contrary direction.

It was soon declared that, in violation of the rights of the defense, a secret document had been submitted to the military judges of Dreyfus; that it had determined their verdict, and that neither the accused nor his lawyer were in a position to disprove it. This act seemed to me to create a presumption in favor of the Captain; what need of new secret proofs if previous ones sufficed? This method of reasoning did not affect my Logician, except in the domain of pure abstraction, and one could not tell if it were applicable to the case in point.

The illegality which was shocking to me, seemed in itself to justify a revision of the trial. He contended that this illegality might spring from interests higher than those of the defense, and that a revision should not be suffered except for more peremptory reasons.

It was known that Dreyfus had been condemned thru the examination of a memorandum written, it was claimed, by his hand, and stating the number of documents delivered to a foreign power. When this memorandum was published in the press, it was found that the handwriting was strangely like that of another officer, Commandant Esterhazy. A large number of experts affirmed that the handwritings were identical. The Logician replied: "What do they know about it? They only worked on facsimiles."

It seemed to me that the motives had never been clearly set forth, which would have explained the crime of Dreyfus; on the other hand, Esterhazy was a gamester, and letters written by him were known to have expressed the wish that France might meet a new Sedan. My friend replied that Esterhazy might be a scoundrel and Dreyfus be none the less guilty. And then were those much discussed letters authentic?

If Colonel Picquart was to be incriminated in a forgery or in the use of forgery which showed that the General Staff shielded Esterhazy, this accusation presented nothing very strange; but if it could be proven that Commandant Henry had committed a forgery in order to prevent revision, this forgery became the patriotic act of a devoted soldier, who, knowing of documents which could not be seen without danger, had no other aim than to produce an equivalent.

What gave me pause in this reasoning was that it was irrefutable if one admitted the inherent premise which was nothing else than a tacit vote of confidence in the military tribunal and the officers of the staff. But this confidence, so far as my friend was concerned, had in it nothing of superstition; it was, he said, confidence in the only men who were informed. On the one side he saw specialists who knew; on the other side, amateurs who guessed. Between the two he did not hesitate in making his choice.

For a long time I was hesitant in my choice; then I was so no longer. For those, whom my Logician called amateurs, those who, according to his point of view were guessing, according to my point of view —*knew*. We discussed every new incident of the affair (every day brought forth new incidents) and we tried to convince each other. We did not succeed and I was greatly troubled. I could neither doubt his intelligence nor his good faith nor his heart. How was it that he saw error where I saw truth? In his confidence in certain officers, which could be but a tentative attitude of the critical mind, did there not enter, without his being conscious of it, something instinctive and mysterious? And I myself, when my faith went out to those others, could I maintain that nothing within me stood between my judgment and the facts? What were these subconscious forces which caused us to oppose each other? Why did I dread them without defining them? Were they to destroy our beautiful friendship?

We might well fear it, for all about us old bonds were being loosened. You may read the story of the "Affair" in your history-book. That which you will not find therein is the accent of passion to which it gave expression. At the Sorbonne the classes resolved themselves into meetings, and in the salons the evenings ended in pugilistic encounters.

Streets were frequently guarded. Long lines of civilians or of soldiers kept the crowd in check which in turn spat upon the villains or the heroes. These civil discords destroyed happy friendships, and even the peace of the simplest homes. Whether one were for Dreyfus or against him, one was always the enemy of someone, it might be of one who had been a friend for fifty years; it might be of a brother or even of a father. For underneath the drama of the "Affair," secret and long drawn-out, another drama was being enacted which combined in hatred two conceptions of society, of life, and of the world.

The most clearly visible aspect of this hidden conflict was the battle waged against Israel. Dreyfus

being a Jew, certain *anti-Dreyfusards* held all Jews
responsible for his crime, and for the disorders in
the country which their determination to exculpate
him provoked. Even if his innocence could be proved,
the Jews were blameworthy in desiring to exonorate
him. The honor of a Jew was as nothing compared
to the safety of a nation. If thoughtful men without
religious affiliation, if some Christians, some Catho-
lics, even priests (and some could be named) enrolled
among his defenders, they were undoubtedly cor-
rupted by Jewish gold or by the Jewish mind.

It was said that an enormous syndicate had been
formed, the *Syndicate of Treason,* the funds of which
were contributed by Jews thruout the world, to aid
those who plotted to disarm France in order to de-
liver her to her enemies. And this was said not to
be unique in the world's history. Wherever the Jew
had appeared, he had brought about ruin. He had un-
dermined the Roman Empire and was in league with
the barbarians at the time of the great invasions. Because of him, Spain of the Visigoths had yielded to
the Arabs. Because of him, the Poland of Poniatow-
ski was dismembered. In the Middle Ages, he had
extorted all the gold of earth thru usury, and then
made use of it in 1789 to finance a profitable Revolution which camouflaged him into a citizen everywhere, and permitted him to realize his dream of

villainous domination thruout a debased century, over the dirty rubbish-heap of a vanished order. Greedy, sensual, a thief and forger, the Jew was a traitor by choice and by his very nature, and if Dreyfus needed a motive for his crime the one fact that he was a Jew explained his treason.

This philosophy of history in the invective vein could not affect me. In vain did I search thru the most secret recesses of my subconscious being. I did not recognize myself in this portrait of the Jew. I was quite sure I was not planning any sinister project by which the world might be overwhelmed. Without feeling myself affected, I was nevertheless unnerved. This anti-Semitism was a new experience to me.

When very young I had heard tell of course of the massacres of Jews in Russia which followed the assassination of a Czar; of women disemboweled, of old men buried alive, nursing babes plunged into petroleum and then thrown to the flames. For a time these memories had haunted my nights, but after a time they faded away.

Then, too, I had often heard tell of 'rishus.' [1] This word, borrowed from the Hebrew jargon of Alsace, expressed the ill-will of Christians toward Israel. But I was able more than once to prove that the ef-

[1] *Rishus,* Judaeo-German term for anti-Semitism.

fects attributed to this sentiment could be explained by other causes, and the story of the two Jews at dinner and the draught, so jocosely related by our Rabbi, had always seemed to me symbolic in this regard.

My mother, who was French by birth, had often told me that Jews were happier in France than in any other country, and that we must cherish the generous people who were the first to give them the rights of citizenship and had honored a Jewish minister, Cremieux, with a national funeral.

Later there was a great sensation over a book, *La France Juive*, which in most virulent language attributed all the misfortunes of the country to Israel. But I was told this was a pamphlet of hate, and so it remained unimportant in my mind.

Ever since my coming to Paris, because of the scandalous Panama Affair, certain daily papers had thrown themselves into a campaign sponsoring this thesis. But was I reading these papers at that time? I was living in the country which the clamor of the outside world did not reach, and such vulgarities did not seem to me to be worthy of the attention of a mind occupied with transcendental speculation. Finally, why should I pay attention to the enemies of Israel? Was I the guardian of Israel? Was anyone in my circle interested in Israel? Did my school-companions see any difference between themselves and me? For them as for me, Jews had ceased to exist.

Even in my own family which had been so attached to the old rites and ceremonies, these fell into disuse one by one. Without shock, without discussion, without dramatics, thru the simple pressure of surrounding forces, new exceptions were made from year to year to the once revered rules. When I returned to Geneva on my vacation, I perceived some progress each time in the process of disintegration; the festivals were less rigorously observed; the ceremonies were less often repeated; even ham became an item on the menus, and to the horror of Lisette the old Catholic cook, who in other days had insisted on my saying my prayers in Hebrew, and who now alone preserved respect for dietary laws, the lean and the fat succeeded each other in reverse order, and the two dishes finally became one.

Since then at my own patriarchal hearth, Israel had already become so faint a memory it was bound to die in others as it had died within me, and there was nothing left to do but to let it die.

Why then was my irritation against anti-Semitism increasing day by day? What had I in common with those who were being attacked? What was it to me whether these attacks were justified or not?

Would not this pain be at least a fugitive pain? Or, was I to pay heed to the insults of pamphleteers unequal to a really understanding outlook? I might perhaps have calmed and contented myself and shrugged my shoulders after a while, had not my Logician provided a new surprise for me at this juncture, by stating that without following this controversy to the letter he was less certain than I was of its unimportance. It is true that his thought reflected many points of view, but was marked by such sincerity that it compelled me to reflect.

He said to me that the word anti-Semitism served as a label for the most diverse tendencies, the most negligible being that which came from Catholicism as a religion, and that no doubt the most formidable adversaries of the Israelites on the ground of religion would be found among the Protestants.

The most popular of possible acts has always been spoliation of those who held possessions. Some imbeciles and some villains, with the blind assistance of some most honest people, have always known how to persuade the masses that all their ills were caused by the Jews, and that everything that could be done to hurt them was legitimate, even unto pillage and massacre. And, he added, one must not forget the sentiment of a people which sees itself very nearly governed by a low-type minority, by a race which this people had habitually (why—did not matter to-day) despised for many centuries.

He recognized that Israel had its idealists, its Utopians, its mystics for whom Jewish interests did not count, but he saw only in these sublime spirits poor politicians, for they builded in dreams while we live in reality. He did not deny that certain Israel-ites, more intelligent than the average man, might render greater service, that they might on occasion prove themselves even greater patriots than other people But to his way of thinking too many Jews filled too many places, since the first crisis revealed the survival of their solidarity and their narrow con-ception of nationality.

Thus wishing to show confidence in those who were appointed to the administration of his country, and to find in them interest in and sympathy for his coun-try, my dear Logician had not found it illogical in himself to believe that, without absolutely excluding Jews from every public function, they were only to be allowed a voice in the State proportionate to their numbers in the nation.

I was stupefied. Did Jews really govern France? Was it indeed necessary to deprive them of the rights they now had—the rights they had won? Was it because of their solidarity that Jews believed Dreyfus to be innocent?

How could a lucid and passionless intelligence conceive or accept such hideous conclusions? I could find no answer and could not divert my mind from seeking one.

It was a sad night on which I suddenly realized that accord between my friend and myself was no longer possible, that our misunderstanding had not its origin in facts, nor in their interpretation, nor in the conclusions more or less cogent, which we had drawn from them, but in a reality which had escaped us, more real than we ourselves and very very ancient. Interested at closer range now in the Dreyfus battles, I had signed a protest in favor of Picquart which appeared in the daily press. In his tender consideration, my friend had made me feel that as a stranger or semi-stranger I should have abstained from taking part in this protest. From the viewpoint of pure logic he was not wrong, but I tried to persuade him thru a letter to the contrary.

Admit,—I wrote him—for an instant that all those who signed the protest had excellent reasons and that those same reasons were my reasons. Did I in signing arrogate to myself a right that was not mine? Do I violate any French law in expressing my opinion, my personal feeling, my pain and my indignation? There is no question here of a political matter but of a judicial matter. I claim that there

is an abuse of power and tyranny in the application
of the law. Strangers who live in France are liable
to suffer under such conditions as well as the French
themselves. Will you reply that they can go away?
Yes, if it were the legislation itself which annoyed
them; but, on the contrary, they may remain and
protest in the presence of an illegal act which plunges
them and with them a large number of the French
people into consternation.

Having the right to protest, I added, I made of it
a duty, believing myself obliged to express an opinion publicly that I had not concealed from my comrades. That the attitude of the ministry was hostile
toward the school was well known, and if disciplin-
ary measures were to be taken against the protestants, it would have been painful to me to be omitted.

Thus I reasoned after the event, but I did not reason about it while signing the protest. I became a
social being; for the first time I took action, and I
believe that action does not only result from clear
reasoning intellectually developed, but often from a
strange impulse the origin of which may be obscure.
I felt that my dilettantism was only superficial, that
I had need of justice, that those humanitarian interests that I had derided were my very own, that
life would never give me sufficient proofs to the contrary to cause me to doubt certain age-old theories,

though seemingly childish and overstressed and even voiced by imbeciles.

Was there then mingled with this human solidarity a Jewish solidarity which made the drama I was living thru more tragic? I could no longer doubt it. But what difference did that make to me? I could neither resist the call of the one nor of the other; both took possession of me as part of my very being.

And I looked upon my friend who seemed so different, so distant! Had we not been in agreement so long because I had been ignorant of myself so long? Did the constraint that I so often felt in his presence reveal a chasm that could never be bridged over? Must that which had united us be renounced? Gentle as was his friendly reproof, did it not shut me out from his country and from his friendship at the same time?

And, while I was weighing and measuring these unhappy thoughts, the "Affair" was becoming a personal challenge to me. My transcendent egotism was fast disappearing. I awaited the morning papers in agony. I read them as tho the fate of this man were bound up with my fate, with the fate of his entire race, in which, little by little, I discovered my own place His letters were published. Beneath the poor declamatory style I heard the cry of tortured innocence. And reaching me across the sea, this cry

clutched at my throat and tore at my heart. At night
on my bed I thought of the prisoner. I saw him alone
on that tropic rock encompassed by the malign silence of his guards. He too was abed in the night fet-
tered to a straw pallet by two iron clamps. And without moving he cried out—he cried out. And his cry
reawakened other cries I had heard long ago, those
of the far-distant pogrom I had been told of when
a child. They again became present, those vanished
figures; the disemboweled women, the old men buried alive, the infants thrown naked into the flames.
And I longed to rise and cry out in my turn, to cry
their martyrdom aloud to the whole world.

And when Dreyfus was recalled from the island
by his judges at Rennes and condemned for the second time my life stood still I could take no food. I
felt myself banished from the brotherhood of man.
And I asked myself "Jew, what is thy place in the
world?"

II

The friendship which bound me to my dear Logician withstood this torture. His tact had proven itself
stronger than my nervousness. Why, said he, should
we quarrel because we differ? Cannot we try to understand one another without trying to be in per-

fect agreement? Our conversations shall no longer be dialogues, but successive monologues Each of us will express his thought without trying to convert the other. Perhaps that will be a finer type of unity. Such friendships have been known. And in fact all shyness vanished; conscious of our differences we became friends who could frankly express our thoughts unreservedly to each other. And in the joy of our new affection, he confided his new thoughts to me which helped me to clarify the confusion in my own mind.

Now having descended as I had from the serene regions where our dilettantism had flourished, he admitted that if science is a vain thing, the repetition of this axiom is vainer still; that if we cannot achieve certainty concerning the meaning of life or of ethics, it were more sensible to accept a way, however arbitrary, than to trust oneself to the more or less logical caprices of one's personal sensibilities. He aspired to lead a social life and was disposed to accept its demands. Upon what then could so logical a mind base its action? Unacquainted with revolutionary tradition as with every other tradition, he could not accept the Evangel of the *Rights of Man* proclaimed by the French Revolution, as a demonstrated truth on which the entire political philosophy of modern society had been made to rest. Following the criticism of Comte, Taine, Renan and Barrès, he only found in this philosophy, mystic outpourings towards vague entities, arguments from hypotheses that were absurd, and an attitude of pity which was either barren or productive of hatred.

And that which irritated him particularly in the "Affair" was that the *Dreyfusards* drew from this revolutionary Evangel, supposed to be beyond discussion, the very substance of their debatable intervention. In one word, humanitarianism seemed to him to call for an act of faith, which did not demand more of our reasoning faculty than any other philosophy of life.

What certitude then remained to him? None save that indefinable heritage from the past which had become a part of his tastes, of his feelings, of his nerves, that something I know not what, which makes a Frenchman feel a closer affinity with a Frenchman than with a German or even with a Swiss or Belgian. Unable to find support in any one principle he harked back to a tradition, to the tradition closest to him, the form of which was least foreign to his nature, to that from which he himself had evolved and which he chose because it was his very own. In fact, he now adopted with all his heart the ideal of country which he had formerly criticized as narrow and vulgar, and which now seemed to him more vital, more important than that of humanity! This being granted, there remained but to reason clearly about the facts of French history in order to deduce the future grandeur of France, by applying to the present conditions those rules of action upon which its past had been built up.

Rediscovering in this way a whole world basic to his instincts, my friend in his great goodness moved me to undertake a parallel task touching the traditions which I had inherited from my race in order to regain that inward peace which I had lost. All things led me to follow his advice. Since the beginning of the Dreyfus Affair, the Jewish question had seemed to me a living thing. Now it seemed a tragic thing.

What, then, is Judaism? A danger they tell me to that Society of which you are a part. What danger? But to begin with, am I still a Jew? I have forsaken the Jewish religion. Just the same you are a Jew. How? Why? What am I to do? Ought I to commit suicide because I am a Jew?

At times I regretted the narrow and rigid faith of my forefathers. But, confined in their Ghettos by contempt and hatred, they at least knew why they were Jews. I did not know. How was I to know? Touching Israel I knew nothing. And I regretted

my years at college spent in the study of philosophy,
Germanic culture and comparative literature. I
should have studied Hebrew, learned to know my
race, its origins, its beliefs, its rôle in history, its
place among the human groups of to-day; to at-
tach myself thru it to something that should be I,
and something more than I, to continue thru it
something that others had begun and that others
after me would carry on.

And I said to myself, if I were to make a different
use of my life, if I were to give myself to other
studies, if later in life I were to have a family without being able to leave my children the legacy of an
ideal that had been handed down to me from my
ancestors, I should always feel a dim remorse, the
consciousness of having been faithless to a trust.
And I thought of my father no longer living, and I
reproached myself for not having appreciated that
Jewish wisdom which he commended to me, and
which lived in him. I reproached myself for my
failure to find any bond between Israel's past and
my own empty soul.

*　　*　　*

It was then that I heard Zionism mentioned for
the first time. You cannot imagine, my child, what
a beacon light that was. Consider that at the time

of which I write to you, the word Zionism was never mentioned in my presence. The anti-Semites accused the Jews of constituting a nation within the nations; but the Jews, at least those whom I met, denied this. And now behold, the Jews were declaring: We are a people as others are; we have a country as others have. Our country must be given back to us.

I now learned that the Zionist idea had its remote origin in ancient prophecies; the Bible promised their return to the Holy Land to the dispersed Jews; thruout the Middle Ages they lived but by their faith in this promise; in the XVIIIth and XIXth centuries great souls, Maurice of Saxony, the Prince de Ligne, Napoleon, had foreseen the significance from the philanthropic, political, economic, religious and moral points of view, that a Jewish re-gathering in Palestine would have. Since 1873 colonies had been established and developed there and finally a new apostle, Theodore Herzl, summoned the Jews of the whole world to create the Jewish state there. Was this the solution I sought? It explained many things. If truly the Jews were only a nation, one could understand why they were looked upon as Jews even when they ceased to observe their religion, and one could also understand why the nations that had sheltered them might accuse them of not sharing their national interests.

The Zionist ideal thrilled me by its loftiness. I admired in these Jews, and wished I could have admired in myself, this fidelity to the ancestral soil which had endured two thousand years; and I was thrilled by the vision of the exodus which would take many of them back from their various places of exile to their regained unity.

My *Logician* on his part approved of my enthusiasm. He saw clearly that my Zionism would, in the end, be in accord with his growing nationalism, accepting certain consequences that would be anti-Semitic. Thus our two minds had in a way travelled in parallel lines, both of us leaving behind us the vision of humanity for that of country—country for me being the Jewish land. But from the beginning I again felt confusedly that my logic was less precise than his, and that if I wished to be, according to my custom, honest with myself, it would not be possible for me to accept his entire process of reasoning in all its harshness.

The third Zionist Congress was about to open at Basle. I decided to attend it. My knowledge of the German language made it possible for me to follow the debates rather closely. Theodore Herzl told of his efforts to obtain a charter from the Sultan. The Executive Council reported that one hundred thousand Jews were already enrolled in the movement and inferred that at least five hundred thousand Jews thruout the world were already Zionists. A plan for Jewish colonization in the Island of Cyprus was rejected as opposed to the plan of colonization in Palestine. The thesis of certain opponents of Zionism who saw in the movement a danger to non-Zionist Jews was refuted.

I heard many gifted men endowed with eloquence and faith, but I was chiefly an observer. What different types of Jews there were all about me: this pale Polish Jew with his prominent cheek bones, that German with spectacles, this Russian with the angelic expression, that bearded Persian, the clean-shaven American, the Egyptian with his fez, and that dark phantom, enormous in his great caftan, with his fur cap, and the blond curls falling from his temples. And in the midst of all these strange faces, something happened to me that was bound to happen; I felt that I was a Jew, essentially a Jew, but I also felt myself French, a Frenchman of Geneva, but French.

It was now certain that the Zionist program in no way implied the return of all Jews to Palestine—a thing numerically impossible, for the Jewish country only offers itself to those Jews who feel that they have no other country. French on my mother's side, my soul and mind were turned towards France, at first when very young thru the gratitude of my parents as Jews towards that country. Later thru my own literary aspirations, and thru my prolonged life in Paris in the midst of college youths and students at the Sorbonne and at the Normal Institute whose friendship and affection had helped me to be myself; and finally thru the anguish that the Dreyfus drama caused me because of France which was lacerated and torn over it.

In my thoughts I could not separate the place of my birth, Geneva, from the great Fatherland of the spirit to which Geneva itself in so many ways belonged. When then, abandoning the egotism of the dilettante, I searched, as did my *Logician,* for a tradition in the depths of my own being, I found there, more powerful and more vital than my Jewish instincts as yet barely awakened, the French tradition mingled with that of Israel.

What then was Zionism to me? It could arouse me, as it still does, this great miracle of Israel which affects all Israel; three million Jews will speak Hebrew, will live on the soil of the Hebrews. But for the twelve million Jews who will continue to be dispersed thruout the world, for all of these and for me, the question, the tragic question remains: What is Judaism? What ought the Jew to do? How be a Jew? Why be a Jew?

III

The reply was slow in coming. I could not invent
it. It must be searched for, searched for thruout
the history of Israel, from the mythical days of the
Bible up to the latest hours of the present time.
This task would demand years, perhaps a lifetime. I
was like Taine when, face to face with the necessity of voting, he found himself constrained to write
his book *The Origins of Contemporary France,* in
order to arrive at his own conclusions. But I was
not Taine. I lacked courage. I was dominated by
other ambitions which demanded less austerity. Literature and the theatre attracted me. I could not
resist their appeal. But the unanswered question
came back to me ceaselessly. How be a Jew? Why
be a Jew? And ceaselessly together with it came the
reproach of my conscience to my indolence which had
not made reply. Some years passed. I saw my dear
Logician frequently. Passing from nationalism to roy-
alism, his way of thinking had developed harmo-
niously, and comparing it with my own disordered
way, I suffered. Every morning I read two articles in
a daily paper which still appears; the one set forth
the doctrine of integral nationalism in clear terms

and perfect language; the other translated this doctrine with prodigious inventiveness into silly insults accompanied by coarse epithets. These insults,
almost all of them, were leveled at Jews, and being
leveled at Jews, they were leveled at me. Each
morning I read this paper; each morning I swore I
would not read it again; each morning, as on the
day before I read it again. And the reading of it
each morning left me in a state of wrath and dis-
tress.

I married. My son was born to me, he whose son
you are to be my child. And then a strange thing
happened. On the morning on which this son was
born, by chance I did not read that paper. And
since that day I have never read it. Why did the
birth of my son liberate me from this nightmare?
I did not know. But when he was one year old,
something else occurred that was not less surpris-
ing. One of my plays had just been produced with
some success, and there were many reasons for me
to persevere in my work. I abandoned it all and
without cessation for three years I studied Judaism.
I believe that I now understand the power that
spurred me on, and the hour chosen for its exercise.
Even then without a doubt, I was obeying the instinct which to-day dictates this book for you. I
may not teach my children the religious practises of

my fathers, nevertheless, I would transmit to them something of Israel.

*   *   *

Is there an ancestral memory? I can no longer doubt it, because that which I then learned seems to me not to have been learned at all but to have been remembered. To begin with—Hebrew. I will never know it as I should wish to know it! But I know enough of it already to be convinced that one cannot understand Israel without understanding Hebrew. Those words which I so often heard pronounced in my childhood, those strange syllables the meaning of which remained a mystery, suddenly opened out to me as doors to a treasure house. And it was not alone their significance which brought me light but the soul that emanated from them. This soul reflected a whole world, the world of my father, my own world, in the evident relation of derivatives from the same root; in the rudimentary structure of the phrase, in the illogical incoherence of images; in the lack of power to express pure abstraction, in the uncertain contours of the verb hardly distinguishing past, present and future, but which seems to move in the realm of eternity.

*   *   *

I desired to know the religious thought of Israel. Better than any commentaries could, some notes written in the course of my studies, will show you what were my doubts, my surprises, and my joys upon that discovery:

The chosen people! . . . The mission of Israel! Israel have a mission and others not have one? Why?

*　　*　　*

They want a God all to themselves; the God of Abraham, of Isaac and of Jacob, the God of Israel! He makes a covenant with the Patriarchs! He renews it at Sinai with their descendants! A pact binds the Eternal to these people for eternity!

Who is this God? An idol? A fetich? The God of a tribe of savages? The God of Israel alone? . . .

But no. He calls the Egyptians his people. He calls the Assyrian the work of his hands; the prophets of the Gentiles have knowledge of him, the Talmud forbids the interruption of the idolator at prayer before his idol because tho he know it not, it is to this God that he addresses himself. Before speaking to Israel this God spoke to Noah, gave commandments to the whole human family. He created the heavens and the earth. He is the one

God, the God of all men, the God of the whole world.
Why then the God of Israel?

I do not understand.

*   *   *

And their Torah, that law which separates them
from all other peoples! They do not labor as others
do; Moses forbids them to yoke an ass and an ox
together at the same plough; they do not sow as
others do; Moses forbids them to sow two kinds of
seed in the same field; they do not reap nor harvest,
they neither build nor reckon, they neither eat nor
pray as others do; they are different in their ap-
parel, in their head-dress, in the unshaven corners
of their beards, in the badge of the covenant on their
flesh. One people separate from all the rest of humanity. What intolerable pride! And this same Law
is supposed to contain the Eternal Wisdom? To
violate it would be to shake the order of the Universe? God consulted it when he created the world?
God himself studied the Torah?

I do not understand.

*   *   *

Their sages say: *The Bible speaks the language
of man.* No doubt they mean by this that God only

revealed to the prophets themselves that which they could understand concerning him, and in language they could understand. This would explain and justify in one sentence all the anthropomorphisms of Holy Scriptures.

*   *   *

Moses at the school of Akiba, what a beautiful symbol! In the Talmudic tale, God shows Moses his disciple Akiba before his death, who will live nearly a century after Jesus. The prophet seats himself in the last of eight rows in the School of Akiba, and listens to the Rabbi's lesson. Akiba comments upon the Law of Moses, Moses does not recognize his own law; none the less it is the Law of Moses.

Divine revelation which came to the patriarchs and the prophets will continue thru tradition, and this continued revelation will only speak to each century in the language that it can comprehend; its mode of utterance will develop as it purifies itself in harmony with the human conscience.

The Bible then does not suffice. As the New Testament does not contain all of Catholicism, the Old Testament does not contain all of Judaism. I must know the two Talmuds, the Zohar, Juda Halévi, Gabirol, Maimonides, all the great thinkers, all the great scholars of the Synagogue. If not I shall know nothing.

*　　*　　*

I believed this Jewish God inaccessible, enveloping his omnipotence in clouds and thunderbolts in order to keep mortals at a distance. And in the tender outpourings of the Psalms I find him as close to me as in the early days of my childish prayers. The patriarchs speak almost familiarly with him; Abraham bargains with him, Akiba, Ben Sakkai, Nahum de Gimso, Rabbi Chanina, Rabbi Meir, all Israel's sages, live in His immediate presence. Is there need of a mediator between this God and Man?

*　　*　　*

Another arresting thought! Jesus pardons the sinner who repents, him who knows not what he does, but he lashes the money-lenders from the temple with a whip of thongs, and hurls maledictions at the wicked Pharisees, maledictions that are equal in vehemence to those of the prophets. The God who chastises is then not absent from the New Testament!

Will the God who pardons be found in the Old Testament?

* * *

He is there! The God of Israel, the just and avenging God is also God the Father, the God of love, the God of forgiveness. He pardons unto the thousandth generation; His justice is ever tempered with mercy; He does not punish unless the measure overflows and chastisement alone can teach repentance—penitence; he who brings to him a contrite heart touches him more deeply than if he brought all the offerings of earth. And if the history of Israel be that of his chastisements it is also and still more that of his forgiveness.

* * *

"Thou shalt love the Eternal thy God, with all thy heart, with all thy soul, and with all thy might." This utterance quoted by Jesus was *first* spoken by Moses.

* * *

How? The entire Lord's prayer: *Our Father who art in Heaven . . . Hallowed be thy name. . . . Thy kingdom come. . . . Thy will be done on earth as it is in Heaven. . . . Give us this day our daily bread. . . . Forgive us our trespasses as we forgive them that trespass against us. . . . Lead us not into temptation. . . .* Each one of these sentences spoken by Jesus when he prayed is a Jewish sentence.

*   *   *

Where then is the difference between Judaism and Christianity? I have been told it is the love of one's neighbor. Is this a great Christian discovery?

Certainly not The Hebrew of ancient times was bound to use well his slave, to liberate him and recompense him at the end of seven years. Not to retain the mantle taken as a pledge, over night; to leave bundles of wheat on his fields for the poor, the widow and the orphan; to *love* the *stranger* as a *brother.*

The Jew of the Talmudic period was commanded to open his door to the poor man as tho he were a member of his family, to be charitable to Jews and non-Jews, to honor the aged non-Jew as well as the aged Jew, to bury the dead non-Jews as well as dead Jews and to comfort those who mourn for them.

"Thou shalt love thy neighbor as thyself." These words also were spoken by Moses.

*   *   *

And then there are these words in the Talmud on the unity of mankind:

"Whosoever is merciful towards his fellow-creature is a descendant of Abraham." Why did God create but one man on the day of the creation? For the purpose of unity so that no man in later times might be able to say to another: I am of a nobler race than thou."

*   *   *

Could then the belief in a future life, in final retribution, be that which distinguishes the one from the other of these two religions? That belief which I do not find in the five books of Moses?

No, for Job proclaims that freed from the flesh he will see God. Daniel believes that those who sleep in the dust will reawaken, some to shame and others to glory. All Jewish prayers are addressed to the God "who quickens the dead"; all the Jews of the Apocalypse call upon the Day of the Great Judgment; all the Jewish sages live in the hope of the life eternal.

Who then, what then, separates you, Jews and Christians? . . .

*   *   *

The Messiah. The Messiah! According to Christians the Messiah has come; the Jews still await his coming!

* * *

Who then is he, this promised Messiah? The Lord's Anointed, the ideal King of Israel, on whom the spirit of the Eternal will rest He will not judge according to that which the eye sees; he will not decree according to that which the ear hears; he will judge the poor with equity and decree in uprightness for the lowly of earth.

After having suffered as his people suffered and taken upon himself the sins of the world, he will regather Israel, dispersed to the ends of the earth, and assure to it a wholly spiritual dominion.

At the end of days the Mountain of Zion shall be placed at the head of the mountains, and the people will flock to it and they will say: "Come and let us go up to the mountain of the Eternal, to the house of the God of Jacob, and he will show us the path, and we will walk in his ways, for out of Zion came forth the Law and the word of the Lord from Jerusalem."

And all the nations will turn their swords into ploughshares and their spears into pruning hooks. And they will never more raise the sword against one another, and they will not learn war any more. "For the mouth of the Eternal hath spoken it."

Such was the promise. Did Jesus keep it?

*   *   *

He thought the end of the world was at hand. He said: "Thy kingdom come." And he believed it had come, this reign of justice, of love and of peace. And he believed himself to be this Messiah, bringing to the world peace and love and justice. But Jews looking about them still saw injustice, war and hatred, and they continued to wait.

Then, in order to bring their faith into accord with prophecy, Christians talked of a *second advent* of which, however, the prophets had never spoken; of a *return* of their Messiah, thru whom all those things should at last be accomplished.

To await his return, is that not to await his coming?

*   *   *

Poor Jesus crucified, over whom I wept in my childhood, adorable Jesus whose bleeding image I could not look upon in the somber chapels without trembling, wast thou then mistaken? And was thy error blasphemy? That Law of which thou thyself hadst said that not one jot or tittle could be changed, that Law that thou didst declare to be holy, did it condemn thee holily? What then was the crime of those Jews who, according to thy own word, knew not what they did, and who rather than salute in thee the Eternal, submitted to death? Sooner than believe that the illimitable could limit himself to a human form, that diety could be a visible Son of the Invisible God, they were ready to spill the blood of the purest of their sons, and to let it flow over them century after century, leaving its stain for all time.

*   *   *

What a gulf between these Hebrew dreamers and the Greek thinkers! The Greeks proceeded by subtle reasoning, the Hebrews by mighty intuitions. At first sight the reasoning seems more convincing; an illusion of discursive thought. Does it not also rest on the disguised intuitions which it takes as axioms and which in themselves possess no logical value?

Why then prefer reason to intuition as a matter of principle and apart from all application?

*   *   *

"Hear, O Israel, the Eternal thy God, the Eternal is One." In the ages when men bowed them-

selves before thousands of gods, and though they
saw in nature the action of thousands of divided
forces of these thousand divine gods, the ancient
prophets of Israel had the sublime intuition of One
God. And to-day science rediscovers this unity in the
universe and shows us in the structure of the atom
and in that of the solar system one and the same
plan, one and the same thought!

*   *   *

I read in the Talmud that God created man and
that "man is free" and in the Zohar [1] I read that
"the word of man created new heavens."

Creation, liberty; two ideas foreign to Greek
thought which are the substance of Jewish thought.
God, creator and free, creates man in his image;
and man freely created in the image of God, in his
turn freely creates!

*   *   *

According to these Jews, God is at the same time
outside of the world and in the world. Outside of
the world, transcendant, he is inaccessible to human thought. Immanent, in the world, he is very
close to us, he is within us. And in the measure in
which it is within us, this divine Presence, this

[1] Zohar—textbook of the Cabalistic Doctrine.

Shechinah, as it is called, finds itself united with the progress of the human conscience The Unity of God, which was broken by being refracted in the diversity of human beings and which was divided in the divisions of mankind, can be restored by prayer and justice which unite men.

A Talmudic sage relates that in the beginning of the world the presence of God dwelt on earth. The sin of Adam caused it to ascend to the first heaven, that of Cain to the second heaven, with the generations of Enoch, of the Flood, of Babel, of Sodom and of Egypt, it rose from heaven to heaven unto the seventh heaven. But Abraham, Isaac, Jacob, Levi, Kehat, Amram, because of their virtues caused it to redescend from heaven to heaven, unto the first heaven and then with Moses it returned to earth.

According to the Zohar, when man sings the praises of God on earth, the angels chant them above; when he sins here, he interrupts the angel choir, when he proclaims the unity of God on earth, he makes it a reality throughout the Universe. Thus man's justice will magnify and fortify the presence of God on earth. Man collaborates with God By a new creation he will perfect the world created by God. His wrongdoing will shatter the divine unity; his good deeds will restore God's unity.

Herein lies the mysticism of Israel. It is not lacking in grandeur.

* * *

Is then this *God-hypothesis* inadmissible?

I cannot understand the motion of the hands on the face of my watch without the intelligence which conceived its mechanism and the will that executed it, and can I then explain the harmonious complexity of the universe as the play of chance and blind forces? Am I not constrained to think that there is somewhere something akin to an intelligence and a will infinitely more powerful than that of man, and by which all things will be made plain?

A long time ago I gave up the childish atheism, even the agnosticism of my first philosophic ambitions. Neither Spencer nor Kant affects me any longer. I no longer believe that mind can evolve from matter even thru evolution, unless matter has first been endowed with the spirit. I no longer believe that the real presence must remain utterly unknowable; to hold it to be unknowable is already to know it to a degree; and if we can, by thinking it, give to it the shape of our thought, there must be some relation between our minds and the real presence.

The great scholars of to-day tell us that science itself is but a vast hypothesis which only provisionally and approximately explains certain aspects of reality. If the hypothesis of God explains other aspects to me, ought I to fling it aside because it is but an hypothesis? The lay-philosophy of Lachelier, of Boutroux, of Henry Poincaré, the philosophy without God, does it not culminate with Bergson in the *fact of liberty*, and the *reality of the spirit*, in *the idea of a God, free and creative?* And is this not exactly the conception of Israel?

How many times I discovered myself reasoning without willing to do so, as tho I subconsciously admitted the presence in myself of this spirit. How often some event in my life was made clear to me, not by those events that had gone before it, but by those that came after, as tho a hidden providence, with which I had made myself a voluntary co-worker, had in my past prepared my future, and had led me to it thru myself.

If this spirit dwelt in me, and in the world, would it not also dwell in world-history? In the history of nations, in the history of Israel? It is conceivable then that certain geniuses, certain races, felt its presence more keenly than others, and that the one that felt it most was conscious of the mission to proclaim it.

Why not?

*   *   *

A Jewish race?

It seems that all the anthropological types are found in Israel: broad-headed Jews, long-headed Jews, white Jews, yellow Jews, black Jews. Could Israel then only be a race in a spiritual sense? Could these different bloods form but one blood because there flowed in them but one thought?

*   *   *

The Torah of Israel. I begin to see more clearly. There are two aspects of the Torah.

I. The moral and religious precepts of justice, of peace, and of love which form the ideal law of all human society, and also the law of the universe. For according to our prophets and our sages, the order which presides over the harmony of the earth and the heavens is of the same essence as the moral order. (And that would explain why: "God while creating the world read the Torah.") II. The special law of Israel; which includes the other but adds to it all the precepts which govern the life of this people and makes it different from other peoples.

Between these two aspects of the Torah there is an underlying unity. In order that at the end of days the Messiah may reign over the world, with his justice, his peace and his love, it is necessary that Israel, which is the hope of the Messiah, shall remain Israel to the end of time. Then its special law must be eternal as is the universal law.

*   *   *

How unjust I had been concerning those six hundred and thirteen commandments, obedience to which is exacted of the Israelite! The religious customs of which I had been critical in my youth were suddenly made clear to me in a magnificent way.

Those Jews desired to connect God with every act of life from the loftiest to the lowliest; to make of each one of them an act of homage to God, thus even spiritualizing eating and drinking and placing daily life on a spiritual plane. Thru ceremonials, thru charity, thru penitence, thru festivals, thru joy, to create, as the Bible puts it, a *people of priests;* not priests withdrawn from the world in prayer or contemplation, but priests taking part in every phase of life, in study and in work, in the family and in society, and sanctifying every act of this life thru prayer and contemplation. A people which should

consist altogether of men like my father! What a
people!

*   *   *

And this is not all. Israel did not desire to be a
holy people for itself alone, but also because of its
mission. Its mission! Egotism? Pride?—Not in the
minds of our prophets nor our sages! Israel seemed
to them a poor and wretched people, full of sin and
ever falling back into sin. God only chose this clay
to reveal what He could do with clay. For this God
of Israel does not belong to Israel He is the God
that Israel, amidst the enmity of the nations, is to
reveal to all men, until the coming of the time when
all nations with it will adore the One God.

In thus charging itself with the burden of His law,
Israel feels itself chosen, not as a master but as a
servant. It only stands aloof from others because
of a duty it has imposed upon itself; it only separates itself from others for the purpose of uniting
them.

There are two aspects of this mission. To proclaim thruout the earth the Name of the One God.
To hope, to wait, and to work toward the end that
with the coming of the Messiah, justice and peace
shall reign on earth.

Monotheism and Messianism; is there a connection between these two ideas?

*   *   *

I see! I see! I have found it! I understand: "Love the Lord thy God." "Love thy neighbor as thyself." It is here that our sages are at one with Jesus. There are two commandments which resolve themselves into one: man being the image of God, to love man is to love God.

"Be ye holy as I am holy," said God to the Hebrews. Man, created in the image of God, must be like his creator.

Thus God being One, man must be One. In his divisiveness here on earth man destroys the Divine Unity. To proclaim it does not then suffice. The Talmud says: "If you would glorify God, try to be like unto him." In order that God's reign may come on earth, man must recreate man created by God, until the unity of man reflects and recreates the Unity of God upon this earth.

According to the Talmudic and Cabalistic commentary on Genesis, Adam—the image of God—was at first man and woman at the same time; conjugal love, a return to this unity, thus becomes a return to the image of the divine unity. Sin multiplied men and divided them; the love of the family, the love of one's neighbor, social justice, which thru union create vaster and ever vaster groups of men, also create more majestic images of the divine unity; and peace among nations will create the greatest of all. "The name of God is Peace." When men, free creators, shall have created Man, "God will be One and his name will be One."

Faith in the progress of man, creating thru his progress the Kingdom of God, this is the faith of Israel. The keeping of His law seems to Israel to be bound up with the coming of the Messiah, and the coming of the Messiah bound up with the perfect man. In order to fulfill this promise, he desires to educate himself, to preserve himself, to make of himself according to the word of the Talmud "a cement" between the nations. He would place within himself, according to the word of Judah Halévi, "the heart of the world," identifying, alone among all the other nations, his destiny with the destiny of all, he would become a nation of priests in order to become the priest of humanity.

The Unity of Man is, therefore, not a logical entity for Israel but a revealed truth, a divine truth, which reaches out to the future from the past, of which the people who proclaim it, in conjunction with all other peoples, must thruout the centuries create a human reality.

The Unity of Man is to the Jew an article of faith as is the Divine Unity, and when I search the conscience of my race to find what my duty as a Jew is, its God makes answer to me: "Thy duty as a Jew is thy duty as a man."

You see, my child, how far distant I now had come to be from my *Logician;* reasoning independently of the Jewish faith, he seemed to me to oppose humanity to his own race; as a Jew I must unite my race with all humanity.

CHAPTER III

ISRAEL ETERNAL

I

I did not doubt that these beliefs were good. But in what measure was I to accept them? They might be but beautiful chimeras.

But even if my mind retained its critical attitude, my heart was moved. What perspectives were opening out! What a past and what a future! Perhaps the dream of this people was an illusion, but what a position this very illusion has given them in the world, and what a place it gave to me also as a descendant of this people!

That which might have left a doubt in the mind of the *philosopher*—which I no longer was—the imagination of the *poet*, which I had hoped to become, dared to affirm. I wanted to dedicate to the memory of my father, who was ever present in my thoughts, a Jewish epic, a kind of *Legende des Siècles*, which would be the epic of the great mission

69

from ancient times to the present day. This is why
the poems were written which make up the first
two books entitled *"Hear O Israel."*

Following the Talmudic tales, I depicted God
considering the future sins and hatreds of men, and
hesitating to create the world; then, in a vision, seeing Abraham, Isaac and Jacob, the three heroes,
arise without arms or an army and saying for their
sake, "Let there be light." I told of Egypt, its war-
riors and its priests accusing the Hebrews before
Pharaoh, of the River of Sighs, of Moses and the
burning bush, of Moses reaching the Promised
Land, imploring God to permit him to live and enter
into it; and of God showing him another Promised
Land, the Land that is to be, when man shall be
One. And I followed the promise of Samson to
Gideon, of Samuel to David. I built the Temple of
Solomon to peace; I saw Jezebel and Zedekiah,
Elijah and Jeremiah; I again lived with them thru
their sins and thru the forgiveness of their sins. I
saw the chastened people dragging themselves towards the Exile. I saw God placing the yoke around
His neck, and the chain about His hands in order
that He might follow His people on their blood-
stained route towards a united humanity.

And I yearned to sing the songs of the Captives
of Babylon, Ezechiel and Nehemiah, the hope of

returning, when the Great War broke out. Can you understand, my child, what I was then experiencing? I had just come to understand with my whole soul all the lyric strain in my race, to live again thru Israel for Israel—and once again, as before at Basle in the midst of the Zionists, I felt I was a Jew, intensely Jewish, but also intensely French. It was an instinctive, sudden, complete revelation. I was still a citizen of Geneva and I joined the Foreign Legion and set out for the front. And this is why, if you are born, you will be born a Frenchman, my child.

It was quite a natural thing to do, for thousands of Jews, more foreign than was I to France, did as I did, and I would not mention it to you were it not that this event put a new and most unlooked-for problem before me: how could I at the same time feel myself absolutely Jewish and absolutely French? How was it that without a doubt German Jews in Germany, Russian Jews in Russia, the Jews of every country in every land felt exactly what I was feeling? This is the Jewish enigma of to-day; I shall not be able to solve it until at a later time.

* * *

Be reassured, my child, I will not tell you about the war; not even my war (which at the end of two

years took me into the civil service at Paris). But
it is needful for you to know what was the great
human hope that assuaged so many horrors.

We were told: this is the last war. And we hoped,
we believed, that it would be the last war. At times
I dreamed of it while standing in a trench, watching the distant shells thru the smoke, and the little
space of earth which could be discerned thru the
narrow crevice of an embrasure. I saw with my
mind's eye all the countries, all the continents, and
everywhere people anxious, confident—all men hop-
ing, waiting for the end of the last war, for the peace
of the whole world, for the Unity of Man.

And, I said to myself, has not the voice of the
prophets cried aloud in the desert? Has the dream
once dreamed by the dreamers of Judea become the
dream of all mankind? Do all men await Israel's
Messiah? How can this be? By what miracle has
this message reached their ears? The Mission? Will
it be thru the Mission of Israel?

And in my thoughts I already wrote the last chant
of the Jewish Epic, *The Wailing Wall* The Wandering Jew stopped before the ancient wall where the
Jews lamented over the ruins of the Temple; but
they did not bemoan the ruined Temple; they lamented the Temple of the Unity of Man, which
man has not yet builded. The Wandering Jew slept,

and in the visions of the night he beheld the whole war; he died all the deaths of all the soldiers, by shrapnel, by gas, by submarine, by airplane. All the mothers of the Great War were weeping for their sons, all the dead of the Great War were rising from their graves, lifting their putrid fists, cursing with their broken lips the anti-Christ who armed their dead bones for a war of the dead thruout eternity.

But across the dream listen to the distant chant. Future generations will build the longed-for Temple, for of fratricide fraternity is born. The wheat for the bread is being brought from every field; the grapes for the wine from every vineyard; the table is set on every mountain, on every plain, on all the oceans. All the races rise and take their places, the Holy Communion of Mankind begins; scattered over the earth, the bones of Adam come together, the blood of all men flows in his veins; in his heart all human hearts are beating. As God is One, Humanity is One.

But again there are wailing voices. The Wandering Jew awakens. At the base of the destroyed wall the Jews still weep; the time has not yet come; they must still wander on.

*　　*　　*

And I also, I awoke from the dream of the Great

War, the whole world awakened—the peace was not
peace; the war continued to be war; men wept;
Jews wept. They had fought for all the nations; all
nations had inscribed in the pages of their glory Jewish loyalty and heroism, and the image of Israel torn
and bleeding became more than ever the image of
humanity. And while my Jewish comrades of the
Legion and their brothers on the Russian front were
dying for the Czar, their parents, their wives, their
children, accused of treason, imprisoned as hostages,
driven out upon the roads in the snow and the night,
knouted, shot to death, hanged, burnt alive, were
dying in Russia by order of the Czar!

After the Bolshevist revolution matters were still
worse. In the silence of the night, I heard not only
the moaning of a degraded captain, on a rock far
out in the sea; the wail that arose to my ears made
me conscious of hundreds of thousands of agonies,
more woeful still than those of the Great War. From
my sleepless couch I saw the counter-revolutionary
armies of Petloura, of Gotschal and of Denikine
advance, shouting: "The Jews are Bolsheviks;
the Bolsheviks are Jews." And throwing themselves upon the unarmed Jews, torture and muti-
late and sabre them in the streets and in the cellars,
gouging out the eyes even of nursing babes.
From Germany to Hungary, from Austria to Rou-

mania, the cry was repeated: "The Jews are Bolsheviks! The Bolsheviks are Jews! They planned the terrible war! They signed the terrible peace! Death to the Jews! Death to the Jews!" And while a new Exodus of Israel in rags and shrouds traversed the capitals of Europe and in agony crossed the sea to find the ports of America closed, all the old calumnies of anti-Semitism, all those murderous myths burst upon the world in a flood of printed pages.

How was this possible? Were all those Jewish heroes who had died for all their countries then forgotten? All those bleeding witnesses to patriotism had then proven nothing? Wherefore did this hatred of the Jew persist which has existed since the existence of the Jews and which will, no doubt, endure as long as they continue to exist?

I wanted to know. I took it upon myself to read those incriminating books and to confront them with the history of Israel, which the preparation of my *Jewish Anthology* had made more familiar to me. I resolved to find this seemingly incontrovertible cause of anti-Semitism. Its discovery might complete my knowledge of Judaism. I was soon able to confute a number of familiar myths, that of *ritual murder*, for example, which was persistently pictured as an authentic custom of Israel, when a hundred times the awful thing has been refuted even by Popes. Then too, the traditional picture of the rapacious Jew, as Shakespeare pictured him in Shylock, ignoring the fact that in the original legend the pitiless creditor is not a Jew, and that the right of claiming a piece of the debtor's flesh dates back not to the law of Moses, but to the Roman law of the Twelve Tables.

I left out of account arguments drawn from certain Talmudic texts, isolated opinions contrary to the general thought of the Talmud and of Judaism itself, and of which it was sought to make articles of faith involving all Jews.

Finally, I eliminated the so-called Christian anti-Semitism. Christ commanded that the Jews be forgiven. According to St. Paul, whose doctrine the Church inherited, their very crime itself had in it something of sacredness, since the salvation of the world began with the sacrifice of Jesus, and Jews must need continue to live to the end of time in order to fulfill their mission in converting the heathen unto the end of days by their example. If Christians have persecuted Jews (and they have hideously done so, and still do) it is because they neither possess Christian virtues nor Christian beliefs; they are still pagans, for one cannot be anti-Jewish without being anti-Christian.

Was Judaism *essentially revolutionary?* If moral, social and international progress mean revolution, —yes; but not if revolution implies violence. Karl Marx, a Jew baptised at the age of six years and an anti-Semite at the age of reason it is true, formulated the theory of communism, which is allied to prophetism thru the nobility of its passion for the disinherited. But as to that which concerns the revolutionary translation of this sentiment, it is an easy matter to demonstrate that the *historical materialism* essential to Marxism, is the total negation of the *historic spirituality* essential to Judaism, and that communism has its origins in the socialism of Proudhon, of Louis Blanc, of Saint-Simon, of Babeuf, who, if they were Jews, concealed that fact well.

In the Mosaic legislation, the soil did not belong to the state but to God and was inalienable from Him. According to this conception a piece of ground could only be sold for a period of time after which it returned by right to its former holders. This conservative measure, which made the continuing inequality of fortunes impossible, far from provoking revolution, tends to prevent it, and no Jewish tradition commands or permits anything whatsoever to come to pass thru the violence of revolution.

Is not the Talmud full of conservative teaching? "Woe to the ship which has lost its pilot, woe to the society that has lost its guide." "Always respect those in authority over thy country." "If the king command thee to overturn a mountain set thyself to work without complaint " The tenth commandment, which forbids coveting the good fortune of another, does it not condemn class warfare by the thought it conveys? Was it not in the Bible that Bossuet found his *"Politique Tiree de L'Ecriture Sainte,"* which establishes the divine right of kings?

Did not the Hebrews wait for the consent of Pharaoh before quitting Egypt and their slavery? Did not the Jews suffer themselves to be butchered during eighteen hundred years without revolting, even without defending themselves? Were they not almost forced in the end to be nearly dejudaized before arming themselves against pogroms?

Could Judaism be essentially capitalistic? The entire Bible, the entire Talmud exalts poverty; Jews give up trade as soon as they can for the culture of the mind; everywhere, in all the universities except when their doors are closed to them thru iniquitous legislation, as in Roumania and Hungary their number is out of proportion to their population in the country. Compared to the great Christian capitalists the great Jewish capitalists cut an insignificant figure; the Jewish proletariat is the most wretched of proletariats.

And, could Judaism be an international organization destined to conquer the material supremacy and the empire of the world for the Jews as promised by some of their sacred books? The persecutions endured by so many Jews thruout so many centuries and even in the century in which we live, prove the absence of an efficient solidarity and lack of organization even for defensive purposes. The empire of the world proclaimed by the prophets must be accomplished not thru financial conspiracy, but thru an altogether spiritual struggle which will lead all of humanity to its highest degree of development.

And finally what weight can be attached to anti-Semitic theses when one sees Henry Ford, the richest and most independent man on earth, after having subsidized anti-Semitism for ten years in Europe and in America, make public retraction, and publicly ask forgiveness of the Jews.

But how could an honest man make such a mistake? Was there no basis for all these contradictory accusations? Yes, one fact, without justifying them, explains them all: Jews are Jews; they wish to remain Jews; always, in all places, even despite themselves they remain Jews.

Then, too, every minority is suspected by the majority which holds those who make up this mi-

nority to be like one another and more united than
those of the majority. Must there be a scapegoat
at any cost? It is sought for in the minority which
is held guilty in its entirety; one Jew has committed treason, all Jews are traitors; one hundred
Jews are Bolsheviks, all Jews are Bolsheviks. Pesti-
lence rages in the Middle Ages—the Jews poisoned
the wells. War raged in the XXth century, the
Jews engineered the war.

This phenomenon of collective half-voluntary
illusion is unanswerable: the empoisoning of wells,
the use of human blood, sorcery and magic, all the
accusations leveled against the Jews of the Middle
Ages by Christians who had come to be the majority, are exactly those with which the pagans, ten
centuries earlier, overwhelmed Christians then in
the minority.

Socially, politically, economically, there is no difference between a Jewish capitalist and a non-
Jewish capitalist: but in fact, or because of his
origin of which some sign ever remains, the Jewish
capitalist is a Jew; he belongs to a minority; he
challenges attention; he crowds out the others;
people notice only him, and desire to notice only
him. If there be a complaint against capitalists,
all capitalists are declared to be Jews. Financiers,
scholars, manufacturers or philosophers, dramatists

or statesmen, conservatives or revolutionists, there
are Jews among them everywhere; they could thus
be accused of everything; they have thus been accused of everything.

I came to realize that anti-Semitism had only one
seemingly valid ground: the determination of Jews
to remain Jews. And was this determination justified? By what right had this people been able to
maintain it thruout the centuries and make it
prevail even to this day? To my mind, in order to
deserve this extraordinary favor of remaining a
separate people while mingling with others, Israel
must be needed in order that its mission should
not seem to be but a beautiful dream of the prophets
and a beautiful theme for the poets, but a definite
fact. This mission, of which I had written with
all my heart, was I to believe in it with all my
mind? And if I believed in it, whither would this
faith lead me?

The history of Israel alone could give me a reply.
This history like all other histories takes its
rise in legend, but what am I to think of it, if I find
it as miraculous in its actual development as in its
legendary origins?

*   *   *

Beside his sleeping flock a shepherd of Chaldea

dreams beneath the stars. A voice speaks to him
saying: "I am the God of Heaven and Earth. Leave
thy country and thy idolatrous father and go to the
land that I will show thee. I will make of thee a
great people and thou shalt be a blessing to all the
families of men." A race springs from him which
lives in slavery on the banks of the Nile, for it
was necessary for the fulfillment of its mission that
this race should know every sorrow. Moses liberates
it and leads it thru the desert for forty years, gives
it a Law which forbids murder, theft, lying, blasphemy, luxury, covetousness—which commands the
love of God and of one's neighbor, which regu-
lates life thru justice, peace and charity—so that it
may become a holy people.

*　　*　　*

Then see this horde on the land promised to it.
It has become a nation; it has kings. But Israel is
unworthy of its Law, again and again it falls back
into idolatry, and thereby to the sin, which includes
all sins; for the living faith in one only God, invisible and spiritual, is the first of the truths it
owes to the world. Its prophets proclaim that it will
perish if it deny its God; and its God in turn
chastens and pardons, even as it disregards or ob-
serves his Law.

It is divided into two kingdoms; the one debases itself beyond redemption, with luxuries and idolatry and carnage; it forgets its God, its God forgets it, it is conquered and exiled; it disappears from the world. The other, quite as guilty, goes captive to Babylon, but its God remains in the hearts of its prophets; its God and the God of all men, for all men were created in his image, and he decrees that the Messiah shall be born of his people for all people, the Messiah of his peace and of his justice who will mould the unity of man after the pattern of the unity of God.

And see how this repentant people finds its recompense; Cyrus, a pagan king, restores to it the land of its ancestors; it returns to it purified of idolatry, and neither Greece with its beauty, nor Rome with its power can turn it away from its God. But internecine hatreds destroy it, and it perishes in a second exile which disperses it to the ends of the earth. Its first Temple, destroyed in order to destroy idolatry, was rebuilt for the divine Unity; its second Temple, destroyed in order to destroy discord, must be rebuilt by the Unity of Humankind.

In accordance with the prophets' word, the truth of Israel begins to spread abroad. Jesus, one of the purest of its sons, said it in most touching language. He said it, believing that the end of the world was at hand and that he himself was the expected Messiah. But justice and peace have not yet come; Israel still waits. And the Christians deify their prophet, and the pagans, accustomed to visible gods, believe they see with their eyes the invisible God of Israel; and so the Christian truth is only half-truth for the Jews.

The Roman Empire becomes Christian. It demands of Jews that they become Christians. But they await their Messiah. The destruction of the Temple takes from them the center of their religious life. They reconstruct it in the Synagogue and in the School and spiritualize it again thru their suffering. Torn from the soil of their own country, they make an ideal country of their Law, attaching to the realization of promises it holds for them and for humanity, the hope of an ultimate return.

And again a new thought springs from the ancient thought of Israel; Mohammed preaches the God of Abraham to the Arabs, and while in its Christian form this God is to conquer the two Americas after Europe, he conquers Africa and Asia in his Moslem form as far as the boundaries of China. But Mohammed binds up with it the apparatus of war, and surrounds it with a sensual paradise in which the Jews do not recognize the God of Israel. And

even as the truth of Christ, so is that of Islam no
more than a half-truth for them.

And so for centuries, in all places where they
live, the inheritors of Judaism persecute the Jews.
Justinian deprives them of civil equality and religious liberty. Sisebut the Visigoth, and Dagobert
the Frank, offer them the choice between exile and
baptism. The Crusaders, the Turks, the Moroccans,
the Russians massacre them; they are driven out of
France, out of England, out of Spain; scourged
and tortured they wait for their Messiah.

But great as is their suffering, countless as are
their exiles, in each century a higher Providence
provides a refuge for them. At first it is in Babylon
under the Parthians; they found their academies,
they edit their Talmud. Then it is in Andalusia, in
Sicily, in Castile, in Aragon, at Narbonne, at Car-
cassonne, at Speyer, at Pavia, at Rome; they create
their own poetry and philosophy, they translate
the Greek thinkers for the Christian thinkers, they
counsel kings, they heal popes, they accompany
Columbus across the Atlantic. And then in Holland
modern thought is born of their ancient mysticism.
And in Poland a new mysticism is born of their
ancient religion.

Luther and Calvin had reread the Bible and

criticism was born. In the century of Jesus the Jews said: "Jesus is not God," and they waited Twenty centuries after Jesus, half of the Christian world will say: "Jesus was not God" and they will return to the One God of Israel.

Rousseau dreamed, Robespierre spoke, Karl Marx wrote, Wilson preached. Ten centuries, perhaps twenty centuries before Jesus, the Hebrews said: "The oppressed is thy brother; the poor, the stranger is thy brother, mankind is One like God." And they waited. Twenty centuries after Jesus, mankind is on the march towards its Unity.

But here again the world took only half of the truth from Israel, for neither Robespierre, nor Karl Marx, nor Wilson repeats the message of the prophets in its purity. Whole-heartedly as they desire to approach the ideal of the prophets, they are still far distant from it because of the terms in which they express it.

Surely for Israel, the moral and social duties of the privileged towards the disinherited and of nations towards one another are not optional; they are absolutely obligatory; the Hebrew word that has been translated into *Charity* signifies *Justice*, and this justice must govern the acts of individuals as well as of peoples. And in the same way the moral code of Israel is one of duties, not one of rights nor of interests. It says to the oppressor: "Thou must free the oppressed." It does not say to the oppressed: "Thou mayest oppress the oppressor." It says to the rich: "Thou owest thy riches to the poor." It does not say to the poor: "Thou mayst take his riches from the rich." It says to the nations: "Turn your arms into peace," but it also says to them: "Establish peace between hearts." Israel affirms thruout the centuries its message of Unity. In the measure in which Israel asserts it, it becomes a reality but in the course of becoming a reality it has become obscure and Israel must make it realizable by repeating it over and over again in all its clarity to the end of time.

Christianity incarnated divinity in the flesh of a man. Mahommedanism connected it with violence and indulgence. Both took from it, in order to make it realizable, something of its spirituality, and in the same way Jacobinism, Marxism, Wilsonism only made human unity popular under a still more confused and superficial aspect. These are the halting places along a road that seeks from the outside to join the path of Jewish Justice and Peace, but this Peace and this Justice in their deepest sense cannot be wholly realized, either thru revolution or by the warfare of classes, or thru the harmonious interests of the nations. For the achievement of Israel's

Ideal it is necessary that the inward progress of man bring men closer to one another.

*   *   *

Is this possible? Has this people given the example of it? Alas, Israel is not yet a holy people. The Jew knows his faults and his imperfections; he outdoes the caricature in those Jewish tales which he himself spreads abroad, he laughs over them but he suffers over them, for nothing is more painful to him, nothing is so hard for him to forgive as a stain upon the honor of the House of Israel.

But with all the ugly things so often inherited from the Ghetto, and which ought to disappear—has he not inherited from the Ghetto itself some beautiful things which ought to persist? He has suffered so much hurt, he has suffered so many injustices, experienced so completely the misery of life, that commiseration for the poor and the humiliated have become natural to him. He has abstained so long from shedding blood—even of animals, even of the human beasts who have massacred him—that the horror of murder has almost atrophied the gesture of killing in him. And he has seen at such close range, in his agonized wanderings, so many men of all races and of all countries, so many men different everywhere and everywhere alike, that he has understood, he has felt in the flesh of his flesh, that Man is one as God is One. Thus a race was formed that may have the same vices and the same virtues as other races, but which is without a doubt the most *human* of all races

Look about you, observe: Christian philanthropy is rarely extended to Jews, Jewish philanthropy is almost always extended to Jews and to Christians; if the Jews seem too prominent everywhere, one finds very few of them in murder statistics. Even their enemies admit this *sense of humaneness,* while they blame him for that, which makes the Jew the instinctive friend of peace among men.

This does not mean that, Christianity, following Israel, has not desired to spread, and has not spread, the same virtues. It is false to say that it has only turned its gaze toward the joys of the beyond, as it is false to say that Israel has only kept its eyes upon the earth. Both the Jew and the Christian believe that in order to enter into the Kingdom of Heaven they must establish Heaven on earth; the Jew awaits the coming of his Messiah; the Christian awaits the return of his Messiah and, as I have indicated in my book *Juif du Pape,* in this expectation there resides the same hope.

The Unity of Man which Israel proclaims, the Church has ceaselessly proclaimed. From its incep-

tion, the Church baptized the slave and the king with the same baptism; the Church to-day installs Chinese bishops while the lay authorities of civilized states refuse civil equality to the yellow inhabitants of their colonies; it is the Church that thru the voice of its great thinkers and its great preachers denounces in the enthroning of nationalism, a new form of idolatry: it was a Pope in the Middle Ages who instituted *the truce of God* in the midst of battle; it was a Pope, in the XXth century, who spoke to the world at war, the loftiest words of peace.

But Israel alone preserved in its pristine purity the twofold message of divine Unity and human Unity, and in the path which leads to its fulfillment it went beyond other nations by virtue of its history, and this advance it must guard for its own sake, as well as for the sake of all peoples. For while these ancient truths as yet evoke but feeble response in the many hearts which are still pagan, they are the very life-blood which causes the Jewish heart to beat.

At the moment in history when this *human sense*, heritage of divine inspiration, so painfully acquired by Israel, becomes necessary to all nations, it happens that the Jews, who lived apart so long, are included as citizens of all nations and bear themselves as citizens. They will keep themselves apart from all peoples; they are the only people to-day that consist of men of all peoples; they were a nation among the nations, to-day they are a Society of Nations, and the pact has written itself in their blood. Their duty is twofold; and I have come to understand the two inseparable commands which dictated my action in 1914: "In every country, even unto the giving of your life, be men of your country; and at the same time be Jews; consecrate to each one of your countries the human treasure which you have received from Israel; and the peace of your countries shall be your peace, and the peace of mankind shall be your peace." Thus did Jeremiah teach Israel its duty, thus will Israel fulfill it.

But lost among the nations, will it not risk losing itself, and with itself lose the ideal which it perpetuates? And now at the very hour when humanity begins to feel its oneness, the return of the Jews to Palestine which, according to the words of the prophets, is bound up with this miracle of unity, begins with it. Dispersed everywhere, Jews will be reunited on the soil of their ancestors, and the soil that the Zionists recreate there; the language which they there learn again, all the effort for their resurrection will make the forgetting of Israel and its ideal impossible for dispersed Jews and for dispersed men everywhere.

And now, my child, turn towards the past, look and bethink yourself. There is but one reproach made to the Jews, and despite all the lies and all the martyrdom which accompanies it, this reproach is justified; they will to remain Jews. Does their past give them this right? Does it permit them to be anything else? See the sublime design which is evident from the beginning and which from century to century becomes more apparent. Did the Greeks declare to the world in advance that they would reveal Beauty? The Romans that they would reveal Law? See this people, howsoever wretched and impure, proclaiming what their history is to be, even from the very beginning See them choose the mission which chose them, and walk with it in the path which they foretold for themselves. See this people of ever-renewed sinfulness, twice exiled and surviving two dispersions, and, as ordained by prophecy, bringing back from its first exile the divine Unity and thru the second exile the Unity of mankind. See it hunted thruout the world, ever nigh to extinction and ever finding some providential shelter which saves it from destruction. See it bearing its truth and, because it wills to keep it pure, spread it thruout the world in flames of light which kindle its own funeral pyres. See it incarnating in its own flesh the two loves which are killing it, even at the moment when it gives itself with them to all the nations of earth. See Israel rebuild the flaming altar of its hope which is the universal hope, so that it yet may survive itself.

And tell me if in this unique history you do not feel the eternal presence of a mind and a will that have ordained its mission to this people and have made its fulfillment possible, in trying it thru suffering, in saving it thru trials, in guiding it step by step from its unhappy past to its triumphant future. As for me, my child, who have so long sought for the evidence of the existence of God, I have found it in the existence of Israel.

*   *   *

I am a Jew because born of Israel and having lost it, I felt it revive within me more alive than I am myself.

*   *   *

I am a Jew because born of Israel, and having found it again, I would have it live after me even more alive than it is within me.

*   *   *

I am a Jew because the faith of Israel demands no abdication of my mind.

* * *

I am a Jew because the faith of Israel asks every possible sacrifice of my soul.

* * *

I am a Jew because in all places where there are tears and suffering the Jew weeps.

* * *

I am a Jew because in every age when the cry of despair is heard the Jew hopes.

* * *

I am a Jew because the message of Israel is the most ancient and the most modern.

* * *

I am a Jew because Israel's promise is a universal promise.

* * *

I am a Jew because for Israel the world is not finished; men will complete it.

* * *

I am a Jew because for Israel man is not yet created; men are creating him.

*　　*　　*

I am a Jew because Israel places Man and his Unity above nations and above Israel itself.

*　　*　　*

I am a Jew because above Man, image of the Divine Unity, Israel places the unity which is divine.

*　　*　　*

At times, my child, when I go thru a museum and stand before the pictures, statues, furniture, arms, crystals, mosaics, vestments, ornaments, coins, jewels, gathered there from all places and all times to hang upon the walls or to place upon pedestals, to be ranged behind barriers and panes of glass, classified, numbered, labeled, I dream that some one of my ancestors may have seen, touched or admired some of these things, in the very place, in the very time, in which they were made for use, for work, for the sorrows or the joys of man.

That door with the gray nails, between two poplars, in the gilded frame, is the door of the Synagogue of Geneva thru which my father entered to pray. And there, that bridge of boats on the Rhine over which my grandfather in Huningen crossed the river. And his grandfather, where did he live? Perhaps while calculating the mystic numbers of the Kabala in his reveries he saw across the pensive panes of his window, the sleds glide over the snow of Germany or of Poland. And the grandfather of the grandfather of his grandfather? Perhaps he was that weigher of gold in the Ghetto of Amsterdam painted by Rembrandt.

One of my ancestors may have drunk from that wine-cup on returning home after listening to the teaching of his master Rashi in the School of Troyes in Champagne; one of my ancestors may have sat in that armchair studded with jade when a Sultan bade him feel his pulse; one of my ancestors may have looked upon a monk in his cowl as he carried this cross of Castile while leading him to the auto de fé; one of my ancestors may have seen his children crushed beneath the hoofs of the Crusader's horse, who wore that armor.

These crowns of plumes, were they placed in the hands of another ancestor by an American savage? These African ivories, these silks of China, were they bought by another on the banks of the Congo or of the Amur, to be resold on the shore of the Ganges or on the Venetian Lagunes?

One of them tilled the plain of Sharon with that plough hardened thru fire; one of them ascended to the Temple to offer his tithe in those woven baskets When this marble Titus was in the flesh, one of my ancestors, chained to his chariot, followed him with bleeding feet in the triumph of the Forum. This bearded magi, with the fringed garment, between these two winged bulls with human profiles—one of my ancestors breathed the dust of Babylon beneath their feet; this Pharaoh of porphyry, with his two hands on his two flat thighs—one of my ancestors bowed himself before his slightest breath, before girding his loins and taking his staff in hand to follow Moses across the Red Sea; and that idol of Samaria, with spherical eyes and triangular jaws, perhaps that was the idol that Abraham smashed when he left his home in Chaldea to follow the summons of his invisible God.

And I said to myself: from that far distant father to my very own father, all these fathers have transmitted a truth to me, which ran in their blood, which runs in my blood; and must I not transmit it with my blood to those of my blood?

Will you accept it, my child? Will you transmit it? Perhaps you will want to desert it. Then may it be for a greater truth if there be one. I could not then reproach you. It would be my fault; for I could not have handed it on to you as I received it. But whether you abandon it, or whether you treasure it, Israel will march on unto the end of days.

LIST OF CITATIONS

.

CPSIA information can be obtained
at www.ICGtesting.com
Printed in the USA
BVHW040203300821
615575BV00011B/503